SWEET WINE AND BITTER HERBS

To Jac, on the eve of
our visit to 'where it all began'.
Best wishes,

Wanda

27th July, 2000

For Sarah, Gideon, Raphael and Samuel

SWEET WINE
AND
BITTER HERBS

Poems on being a Jew
in the Twentieth Century

Wanda Barford

With a Foreword by NAOMI LEWIS

FLAMBARD

ACKNOWLEDGEMENTS

Some of these poems have appeared in the following publications:
The Dybbuk of Delight, The Jewish Chronicle, The Jewish Quarterly,
New Wave Poets, Outposts, Stand, The Tablet, Voices Israel and *Write Lines.*

'Movements on the Lake' was runner-up in the H.H. Wingate/Jewish
Quarterly Poetry Competition in 1991.

I should like to thank my husband, Michael, for his assiduous help
in word-processing my poems; my daughter Jeeda for the cover design;
and my younger daughter Imogen for her eager encouragement
when I first began to feel my way towards writing a poem.

W.B.

The photograph of Wanda Barford is by Fritz Curzon.

Flambard Press wishes to thank Northern Arts for its financial support.

First published in Great Britain in 1996 by Flambard Press
Stable Cottage, East Fourstones, Hexham NE47 5DX
Revised edition 1999

Typeset by Pandon Press Ltd, Newcastle upon Tyne
in association with Mary Holcroft Veitch
Printed by The Cromwell Press,
Trowbridge, Wiltshire

A CIP catalogue record for this book is available from the British Library
ISBN 1 873226 17 9
© Wanda Barford 1996, 1999
Foreword © Naomi Lewis 1996, 1999

CONTENTS

Two Sequences

FOREWORD

Poet and poet's poetry – the human and the word – are they separate? Think for a moment (Tennyson? Hardy? Edward Thomas? Yourself, maybe?) and you will know the answer. No doubt about that answer as you read the poems in the well-titled *Sweet Wine and Bitter Herbs*. So it is a fair start to writing of these poems if I set out (and reflect on) a few facts about the author herself.

Wanda Barford is a (classical) musician, a pianist. She is also a magician of languages, perfectly at ease in – how many? Wait, though. Born in Italy, she was nine before she could speak English. Yet this – in her own words 'one of the world's richest and most subtle languages' – would become not only the language of her daily life, but of her creative choice. And at the core of that choice was the special medium of poetry. Aptly, then, it is through this medium that she fulfils the purpose of her book, admirably described in her own Preface. You could say too that the driving theme, the 'matter' of the book, opens special gates to her maker's craft of words. Maker, of course, is the old word for a poet.

This very personal book is, and is not, her personal story. She did have her share of uprooting, exile, journeying – to where? But she was a young child with both parents when they made their timely escape from Mussolini's Italy. (See her fine poem 'Night Express, Stresa' with its brilliant, reverberating end, achieved by the flick of a word.) The real sense of exile, that of her parents, lives in such poems as 'Enemy Aliens', 'Reading to Each Other', 'Leaving You in Africa' and 'A Boyhood in Izmir'. The dire, one-way journey to Auschwitz was made by her proud grandparents and five younger members of the family (three of them children). 'Moments of a Journey' is an enduring record of that journey.

Every practising writer acquires, even without intention, even unknowingly, an individual voice. What makes a Wanda Barford poem clearly recognisable? The subject matter? Only in a general sense. The facts are constant, but every maker views them differently. It is the daily battle with words (and thoughts) in the workshop or *atelier* of the mind that sets the final statements on the page. Even when she experiments in manner and technique ('Like Grey Gulls' gives a very evident nod towards Auden and MacNeice) the Barford voice is there. Certain characteristics are worth noting though, if you pursue the question above; they are not, in relation to her theme, peripheral. One such is her significant use of *things* – the potency of the unpoetic object in her poems. Sometimes the object (Proust, yes, yes) serves to evoke, to fix an event or scene: 'Beetroot', 'Enemy Aliens' (a hat, a glove), the memorable 'Household Linen'. You could add, perhaps, these lines from 'Moments of a Journey':

> Who'll tend to my *yeshivah*? Gave a Turk
> One hundred lire to protect my books
> (I didn't like his manner nor his looks).

In their cattle-truck context those books could stand for everything – and nothing. But sometimes the *things* are statements in themselves – never more than in the stunning list-poem 'Practicalities'.

Then, on a larger scale, there is the central Barford approach by way of anecdote, episode, fragment of history, memory, the moment held in time. The episode may contain its own comment (it's a difficult area, this), though occasionally a poem achieves much in a seemingly casual, throwaway last line. See the glimpse of a dark tomorrow in the final lines of 'Night Express, Stresa' and 'Household Linen'.

Sometimes she makes her point (Browning-fashion – though I think that this is fortuitous) by way of a double image. The scene, revisited, becomes a darker image of itself. (Something of this is in her Primo Levi staircase poem 'The Shout'.) In the mysterious 'Winter Journey' story and image are so fused that you are compelled to read again. Then again. Only the sudden likeness of the snow to 'the starched cloth of ceremony' moves the poem from (untypical) forest fairy tale and places it back in the known Barford path.

The timelessness of this poem is a reminder that, in entering the experiences of her kin and kind, she does not (in spite of the book's sub-title) keep only to her own Twentieth Century. Her awesome ballad 'The Three Boys' – awesome too in its plainness and verbal simplicity – recalls an episode of Jew-murder in the Vienna of 1181. (The pretext – the disappearance of three 'Christian' boys.) This has its close English counterpart in the sinister Hugh of Lincoln ditty, still found in quite recent English song books. As 'Little Sir William' (or similar title: 'Easter Day Was a Holiday') it was in the Britten/Pears repertoire for years, in spite of raised eyebrows, and, I think, a raised voice or two.

Not all of the poems in this book are of equal quality. But the impact of the whole, and of many separate poems, is a lasting one. Wanda Barford is a true maker of the craft, and in using this craft she has kept Primo Levi's injunction in 'Shema' always in mind. Her ancestors, near and far, who are given so living an immediacy in this book, must be sharing their approval of their poet descendant.

NAOMI LEWIS

PREFACE

Between us, my mother who was born in 1903, my father in 1894, and I will have spanned the Twentieth Century. It has been a positive century in many ways – radio, the magic silicone chip, space exploration – but its morality has sunk to the lowest point man has touched, with the scientifically organised extermination of more than eight million 'unwanted, unsuitable' individuals.

Before the century is yet cold, some are emerging to deny that this Hell ever existed. (Such nefarious claims may have contributed to Primo Levi's tragic suicide.) It is all a construct of the fertile Jewish imagination, they say. Since seven members of my family died in Auschwitz, it behoves me, for their sake and for the sake of all those others, to bear witness before the century passes. I dedicate these poems to them in an act of memory, as Primo Levi bids us do in his granite-like poem 'Shema': *Meditate che questo è stato* [consider that this has been]. Never, never forget; tell it to your children and your children's children.

I seek also to record through my poems the broader experience of being a Jew in the Twentieth Century – the emigrations, the flights, the numberless journeys, the arrivals at unfamiliar places where strange tongues are spoken. And all those unforgettable goodbyes on the station platforms of Europe: 'Goodbye,' they said, 'Goodbye,' and knew they would never see each other again.

And I go further back to probe and understand the links between my ancestors who were forced to leave Spain during the Inquisition, and their descendants who, like my own grandparents on both sides, settled in the more welcoming countries of the Ottoman Empire.

But everything can have a rosy side. Benito Mussolini, by expelling me from his schools and compelling us, as a family, to leave Italy – we went first to Paris where I learnt French and finally to the then British colony of Southern Rhodesia – ensured that from the age of nine I began to speak and appreciate English. It has been a precious gift, a rare privilege to use one of the world's richest and most subtle languages. I savour it every day, turning it around in my mouth as I explore new words, new sounds. It's now the language of most of my poems; it clothes and embellishes their thought, though perhaps their soul lies elsewhere. As I often say: I write poetry in English, not English poetry. Whether there is a distinction will be for the reader to determine. It is a tribute to the versatility of English that at the close of the Twentieth Century, many others, from all parts of the globe, are doing the same.

WANDA BARFORD

9

Writing is a form of prayer.

FRANZ KAFKA

COSMOPOLYGLOT

'Home is where my placenta is buried.'
                                    (Luo tribe of Kenya)

Ha Madame, vous êtes française?
Ma Lei, veramente, dove ha imparato l'italiano?
¿Como es que habla tan bien castellano?

Εὐχαριστῶ παρα πολὺ; tesekkür ederim.
Kanjani wena azi kuruma Chishona?
A-a-a wena inzwe, lo Madam ena kuruma Chishona.

But where exactly is your home? they ask me.

                    *

Home is the line
Between the sea and the sky,
Purple on the horizon.

Home is a tree –
A cedar of Lebanon,
My arms round its trunk.

Home is the tent
My father's arm makes
Over my head with his *talleth*.

Home is where I am.

THE EXILE

I left things dear to me
                in a different land.
When will I go back for them?
                Will they be there?
Will I recognise them?
                Will they have changed?
Will I? Will I still need them?
                Will it be a going back?
Will I want to go back?

I left things dear to me
                in a different land.

A SPRIG OF RUE

'O! You must wear your rue with a difference.'

That I could sit like her!
Legs so far apart, solid, each one
on its statuesque foot
like the mother in a Henry Moore,
and her skirt and apron so taut
across the knees each cap shone through.

Two or three times a week
she came to us balancing trays
spread with the morning's baking;
we'd sit her down
to a cup of Turkish coffee
for her to savour our praises.

She'd been brought to Rhodesia from Rhodes
(the names reassuringly close) by her son
who'd emigrated. She smuggled a cutting
of rue from her pebbled garden and two sheaves
of white corn; these had dried and yellowed
and the rue run riot under the savage sun.

When they found her
spread-eagled on the road
she was unmutilated
but her pastries squashed,
cheese filling and spinach oozing
where the car wheels rode over them.

Behind her ear was a sprig of rue –
she wore it to ward off the evil eye –
its small yellow flowers blooming
and the pungent smell discouraging
the prompt ants from crawling
over her face and neck and ears.

13

A BOYHOOD IN IZMIR

Throughout the war, sitting with your ear to the Philips,
you picked out the voice of neutral Ankara
amidst the crackle of the short waves,
proud you could still understand the language.

Somewhere beneath the sophistication
of later emigrations, was your boyhood in Izmir
where nightly you were rocked to sleep
to the sound of lapping in the Bay.

Many stories you told of those days…
but we children didn't want to hear – part shame,
keen to cover up our origins; part youth's
impatience with the past.

But the tales have stuck, so vividly did you
recount them: there was the great Fire of Smyrna
after which Turk massacred Greek but spared
houses like yours marked with the Yellow Star;

there was the time when you, a young dandy,
sipping *raki* and savouring *mezes* –
as you still did years and countries later –
you, exchanging stories with your pals,

missed the homeward ferryboat across the Bay.
A great storm blew up such as Izmir had never known,
and the ship went down with all on board.
You felt saved for some purpose. What?

And the time when a dark girl with bright eyes
from across the turquoise Aegean, stepped
into your shop and into leather shoes
of your fashioning, and determined you

to seek for her again. And so, having lost all
in the Fire, you went looking for her among the Twelve Isles
and found her in a house hung with vines,
leaning out of a wooden cantilevered window.

*

Now all that's left of your childhood in Izmir
is a sepia school photo framed in tortoise-shell.
You're the pale boy in the middle of the second row –
your honey eyes apprehensive. All the boys in the front
are wearing short black boots – I cannot see if you are.

LEAVING YOU IN AFRICA

For my father Moïse Jacob Simson
born Turkey 1894, died Rhodesia 1962

If it hadn't been so far
I would have come to tend your grave,
to bring you zinnias, cannas, jacaranda flowers –
but how to cross the sea?
And then the dusty journey,
three hot days to the interior.

If I close my eyes
I can see your headstone with the lizards
panting on the rock, I can hear the long grasses
scratch against each other like dry bones;
as darkness falls, the breathy croak of bullfrogs,
and those light-crazed insects
that whirl round lamps like Dervishes.

If I listen with my mind's ear
I can hear your magisterial voice
praising a piece of homework,
or commanding me to kneel
and say sorry for some childish prank.
And your voice would be no louder
were I right there, placing flowers.

If I thought you *were* still in Africa
I'd somehow try to make the journey;
but over the years
in our mind's mind
we took you back to your birthplace,
to the Bay of Izmir, to the sea
that lapped you to sleep as a child.

ENEMY ALIENS

Salisbury, Southern Rhodesia 1940

Only on Tuesdays did she wear a hat,
pinned at a jaunty angle to her nose,
the veil draped softly underneath her chin;
and gloves too, though soon the need arose
to take one off and press her thumb down on the pad.

From behind his desk, the policeman called out
the list of rules: no groups of more than six;
report same day each week; do *not* stray out of bounds;
'and Madame (leaning forward) no funny tricks
or you'll join the other Eytie internees.'

Father in his spotless suit was affronted:
the fingerprint pad was the same
they used for common criminals. All day
he bore a weight, a sense of shame
that made him stern and grey.

Once the Day of Atonement fell on a Tuesday
and registration held off a day or two.
'You're a Friendly Alien now,' the policeman said,
'we know you're not Italian but a Jew.'
Father was relieved, but saw his 'Eytie' friends behind barbed wire.

SUNDAY MORNINGS: THE VIOLIN CONCERTO

I can hear it now
that taut, off-beat accent
at the start of the third movement.

And I can see you on the settee,
tense, sweaty, your eyes closed,
index finger up, conducting;

your impotent will
hoping to absorb
some of the other's courage.

'His grandfather was Dutch,' you'd say,
'*van* with an *a* is not German.'
And we tried to resist his Germanness.

But the passage in the minor key
melted and disarmed us,
showering us with its benediction.

*

When I left for London
you gave me his bust to place on the piano.
Every time I moved he travelled with me

in a shoebox lined with cottonwool.
On one of those journeys
the head cracked at the neck, the plinth too.

It's back together now...
If I put my ear to his mouth
I'm sure I can hear him

humming one of those tunes
from the Violin Concerto we'd listen to
together on Sundays at home

in that strange far-off country,
the veld and the dust closing in on us –
a brother and sister, homesick exiles.

READING TO EACH OTHER

Often, in the evening,
he would read to her in English,
a piece out of the newspaper
or some passage
from a newly acquired book.

There would be difficult sequences
which they'd tackle together,
each offering a possible explanation
until all the meanings
had been carefully unravelled.

His voice was calm then
and as English as he could make it;
her high soprano notes
weaving in and out of his bass
like embellishments upon a ground.

They were close too
when they went for 'their' walks
by the golf-course, arm-in-arm,
at sunset, and returned
just as the light was fading.

THE REVENANT

Tired of eternity
he came back
for the temporal pleasures;
a good sleep, in bed,
a tasty meal and a chat.

He was dressed
in his ceremonial suit,
the one he wore to synagogue
on High Holy Days.

Visiting life
was for him
a celebration.

WINTER JOURNEY

By stealth the snow came, during the night:
it crept up on us while we slept,
though we had known the ushering cold
in our bones, days before.

And we felt it coming from far-back places:
childhood forests of black trees, buried lakes
and those lean wastes
hungry with the howling of wolves.

This morning, here outside the window,
a crisp whiteness has covered the earth
like the starched cloth of ceremony;
when the snow melts, a new journey will begin.

TURKISH BATHS

Rhodes 1934

Roaches crawl round the rim of the sunken basins
      where the water-jets spurt;
the naked women squat or sit
      buttocks flattened by the paving stones.
Their age is in their breasts;
some wash each others' hair,
      pouring water from flat metal dishes.

I ache to run out – feel myself choked
      by the sulphurous smells,
the heat, the sweat, the flesh;
      and repelled by the cockroaches –
blacker, sharper, shinier than I've seen on dry floors.

But my grandmother signals that if I endure to the end,
I'll be rewarded – an extra pastry,
      a second candied apricot –
when we emerge room by cooler room, to the outer island
of polished wood and crisp white cushions
      where coffee is served.

In the rose-water-sprinkled freshness
      of this outermost room,
wearing our clean newly-starched clothes,
      comes the moment of well-being:
we are cleansed of the dirt
      that had penetrated our pores,
we are laved and purified.

FRIDAYS ARE SPECIAL

She's up at daybreak,
punctual as the Aegean sun,
to see her loaves well-risen
and send them off all plump
on their wide baking trays
to the communal ovens.

There's much to do on Fridays:
chickens back from the *shohet*
must be plucked, gutted, soaked
in salty water; biscuit-dough
twisted, egg-brushed, sesame-sprinkled;
apricots stewed till syrupy;
coffee ground fine
in the square wooden mill.

And the visit to the Turkish baths
for the ritual cleansing
while shiny cockroaches
climb the damp walls,
and girls' eyes ponder
the geography of their mothers' bodies.

Then home in fresh clean clothes
smelling of rose-water,
to lay the table
with a crisp-white cloth,
await the setting of the sun,
and light the Sabbath candles.

*

Mother of my mother
was it on a Friday evening
you were marched to the harbour,
stripped of jewellery
and packed into the waiting boats?

Were you in your fresh clothes
smelling of rose-water,
had you put out the fire,
turned off the gas
and hung your apron
on the kitchen hook?

'shohet': a slaughterer of cattle and poultry in accordance
with Jewish law, ensuring the meat is kosher.

BEETROOT

Often, peeling beetroot, I think of you
my old young cousins, and I see your sunken eyes
and those numbers tattooed deep
into your fleshless arms.

Looking down at my stained fingers
I see your rouged cheeks faking health,
turned up to the guards, to plead
they postpone death a while.

The ruse worked for you; but for others
whose cheeks you painted – drained mothers
with pale children – it failed. They shuffled
into the gas-chambers wearing this loud disguise.

FAMILY SNAPS

Here's one of grandfather's garden in Rhodes;
seven of us are in the group,
smiling the forced smile of photographs.

We're in two tiers with little me in front
eager to run off but restrained by a big hand.
My brother has put on his Colossus pose;
an aunt flicks forward two favourite curls.

Our oily skins tell of heat;
in the air orange-blossom and oleander...
not even the mulberries crushed blood-red underfoot
foretell anything but sweet air and everyday sorrows.

But another summer, much like this one,
the people of this garden (and it could have been me)
were pushed into boats and sailed to Piraeus;
then overland by cattletruck to Auschwitz.

My grandfather never got there.
For defying his SS guard
he was kicked to death on the train.

Granny, survivors said, went into the gas-chamber
carrying her soap and towel – she thought it was
a kind of Turkish bath like the one she used to visit

each Friday; I went with her
and when we came back home
it would be time to light the candles.

FROM RHODES TO AUSCHWITZ

A DIRGE

A crow in flight
From noon to night
Saw you descending
Heard your ending
Picked out your bones
Among the stones
Of an alien land
Returned like Ulysses
To bury them
In Aegean sand.

MOMENTS OF A JOURNEY

In July 1944 the small community of Jews that had
lived unmolested in Ottoman Rhodes since the
expulsions from Catholic Spain in the fifteenth
century was deported to Auschwitz by the Nazis.
A ten-day journey in three petrol tankers took
them to Piraeus, thence overland by cattletruck to
Poland. My grandfather, grandmother, aunt
and uncle and their three children were part of that
unhappy band. Grandfather never reached his
destination: for standing up to his Nazi guard he
was beaten and kicked, and died later on the train.

They've thrown us all into three rusty ships,
The young, the old, the sick and walking dead.
That baby's blue from mouth to fingertips;
An old man shivers: is it cold or dread?
We wait to sail. We're all together here.
It's better so, to have our loved ones near.

Where we are headed nobody will say;
Is it perhaps to Kos to fetch out more?
Forgive me God, I'm too distraught to pray.
We'd spent three nights all huddled on the floor
Of that Fascist Palazzo of grey stones.
It's good to feel the breeze search out my bones.

Our island looks more lovely from the sea…
To think I'd sworn never to leave this place,
To die and be interred under a tree,
My *talleth* round me, the earth against my face;
Or up among the eucalyptus groves
Alive with song, the coo of turtle doves.

Look my love, my wife, there's the Mandraki
Where arm-in-arm each sunset we would walk;
Then you would lower your eyes as I sipped *raki*.
How I admired your brightness and your talk...
We're sailing out between the Doe and Deer.
(I've got my keys. God, let us come back here.)

This is the spot where the Colossus stood
The Rhodian sculptor's 'Sun', his boldest work.
Now all's destruction; a barbaric brood.
Who'll tend to my *yeshivah*? Gave a Turk
One hundred lire to protect my books
(I didn't like his manner nor his looks).

Hunger and thirst (not fear) we've learnt to quell;
They've just become a thud inside the head.
The discipline of *taanit* serves us well.
At last we're getting water-barrels, bread.
Now we're in Kos. More Jews to come aboard.
Protect these folk. Protect us all, O Lord!

A storm whipped up some mighty waves last night.
We're drenched. Today the sea's a metal grey.
At dawn an old man died – put up no fight;
The children's friend, a sweetmaker, they say.
We buried him on a deserted isle;
A short *kaddish*, an entry in God's file.

I see Piraeus in the distance now...
We're disembarking to sharp German shouts;
They're ordering me to strip. How can I? How?
In front of women, kids. What kind of louts?
They're beating me with sticks, belts, whips, a chain.
Don't leave me. Put me with you on the train.

*

30

He did return to his enchanted isle,
Migrating with the butterflies in spring;
His spirit free and strengthened by his trial.
(I felt him there and thought I heard him sing.)
And though, like theirs, his body can't be found,
It lies whole, somewhere hallowing its ground.

'Fascist Palazzo': *an Italian Air Force headquarters.*
'Mandraki': *the main promenade of Rhodes.*
'yeshivah': *library or place of study.*
'taanit': *fasting, as on the Day of Atonement.*

TWINS

To the memory of my cousins
Fortunata and Gioia

Two little twin girls
Five years old;
One with a sore throat
One with a cold.

They must get up
And march in the rain
To get to the station
And on to a train.

They get on the train
With their mum and dad
It smells of wee-wee
And things gone bad.

For one whole month
They lurch and they rock
Some grown-ups spit
And yell and mock.

'Where are we going?
We'd like to see out.'
'You can't' sighs mummy
'Keep still, and don't shout.'

At last the train stops.
They hear '*raus*' and '*schnell*'
But what is this place?
They cannot tell.

And mummy goes left
And daddy goes right
And Rachel, big sister,
Holds their hands tight.

They're told; twins are nice,
Should go to Hut 8
Let go sister's hand
And stand up straight.

They trudge to a hut
Set out like a lab;
A clean-looking nurse
Gives each a quick jab.

The sore throat and cold
Get worse in there;
They're given injections
Of pure, pure air.

And their hair falls out
And their skin flakes off;
And they have a bath
In a drinking trough.

They worsen and worsen
And soon they die;
And no-one to bury them
And no-one to cry.

PRACTICALITIES

A FOUND POEM

The crematorium chief at Majdanek
had his own bathroom beside the ovens:
it was hot dusty work in the low-roofed,
iron-clad crematoria. The hours were long.

At Treblinka prisoners were made to do
exercises when they got off the train
to improve the circulation: carbon
monoxide takes effect more quickly then.

The furnace at Birkenau was supplied
by TOPF UND SÖHNE: the side-door by THEO-
DOR KLEIN of Ludwigshafen. The maker's
stamp embossed on the side of the oven.

Block 10, Auschwitz, the Racial Hygiene block;
stubby silver syringes inject phe-
nol straight into the heart. Death guaranteed
in two minutes and twenty seconds flat.

ALEX ZINK paid fifty pfennigs to buy
one kilo of human hair and turned it
into cloth; others stuffed mattresses. Gold
from fillings was taken to the Reichsbank.

AUT of Berlin supplied a two-furnace
crematorium, then a five-furnace one
to 'cope'. It cut incineration time
from one hour to nearly fifteen minutes.

When the crematoria could no longer
cope, great pyres were built fed by the fat of
burning bodies. Nothing must be wasted.
Extra fat was used for soap and candles.

The Zyklon B (hydrogen cyanide 'dis-
infector') was supplied to Auschwitz by
DEGESCH – twenty tons between '42
and '43; kitchens by HILDESHEIM.

*

Human compost endures.
Each winter in the forests
around Treblinka
fragments of bone
wash to the surface.
There's a mountain too
of artificial limbs,
a pretty wooden hand
with the nails etched
and painted pink
on the fingertips.

And the suitcases
carrying the clothes
they would find again
'afterwards'
bear the owner's name
neatly inscribed:
'Else Meier, Köln'
'Simon Rosenberg, Berlin'
'Grete Schwartz, Hollandstraße, Wien'
'Lotte Rapaport, München'
'Norbert und Sigmund Steifel, Frankfurt'.

MY DEAD ONES IN VERONA

A table of German youths
spitting words, borrow chairs;
my grandfather and theirs in black uniform
stood eye to eye across barbed wire.

Dante, over there, pensive,
a pigeon on his head,
knew exile in this city of Verona –
'how sad,' he said, 'to descend another's stair.'

What would he have said
to another's land,
to women without hair,
to gas instead of air?

My dead ones call to me,
call to me, here in Dante's square –
theirs to ascend
theirs the golden stair.

LIKE GREY GULLS

Lac Léman 1937

When I was little I came this way
And it wasn't autumn and it wasn't May.

It was hard December and the hearts of men
Inside and out were colder then.

I came on a train whose wheels went round
With a shriek and a psst…and an aching sound.

We passed through a tunnel dark as night
But when we came out we leapt at the light.

The hotel was cosy and people were kind,
It would have been easy to be deaf and blind.

As I watched coloured windmills on masts on the lake
I couldn't yet fathom how much was at stake.

The saddening willows deprived of their leaves
Curtained the water like cascades of beads.

In rows like grey gulls the refugees sat
To every official each touching his hat.

Disney's *Snow White* was showing in town;
The witch stood for evil (already I'd known).

That night in the room I couldn't find sleep;
I was thrown in a dungeon six million souls deep.

Now the danger is nearing so where shall we go?
Oh where to this time, the vales or the snow?

Neither my dears, it's neither for us;
we shall go off the map, so don't make a fuss.

ROMANY RHYME

500,000 Sinti and Romany gypsies
were exterminated in the concentration
camps of the Third Reich.

Romany, Romany,
Where do you roam?
I've been down to Auschwitz
To visit my tomb.

Romany, Romany,
What did you there?
I saw a gold tooth
And a piece of black hair.

PETITIONS

Into the cracks
in the Wall of golden stone
go the rolled-up
paper prayers of men.

Out of the cracks
in the Wall of golden stone
brightly coloured flowers
grow unbidden.

THE THREE BOYS

A BALLAD

As I was walking all alone
Beside the frozen river
I heard three children making moan
It stayed with me for ever.

Three lively children skating there
Had fallen through the ice
Their bonnets red, their fine blond hair
Had vanished in a trice.

'The Jews, the Jews they stabbed them dead
And bled our sinless mites
For blood in their Unleavened Bread
And other savage rites.'

They stormed into the ghetto then
To loot and burn and break,
They rounded up three hundred men
And marched them to the stake.

But when the cherry blossom came
All pink on Danube's strand
They found the blue-eyed boys, the same,
Untouched by human hand.

As I was walking all alone
Beside the thawing river
I heard three hundred making moan
It stayed with me for ever.

*This incident occurred in Vienna in 1181. In London in 1991,
Lady Birdwood, aged 78, was found distributing leaflets
asserting that Jews had ritually killed Christian children.*

'TODAY I AM AS OLD AS THE JEWISH RACE'
Yevgeny Yevtushenko, 'Babi Yar'

*In 1941, 33,000 Jews were executed by the Nazis over two days
at Babi Yar, near Kiev. In 1961, Soviet police broke up a crowd
of 1,000 Jews who had gathered to commemorate the massacre.
Finally in 1991 the Ukrainian government formally apologised
to the Jewish people for their failure to prevent the atrocities
and allowed the erection of a memorial by the ravine.*

There's a memorial now at Babi Yar
Where first the grass alone received the dead
While SS men made bonfires of the Star.

They'd come with wreaths and candles in a jar,
The shrieks of the machine-gunned in their head.
But no memorial then at Babi Yar.

'I feel I am a Jew; I bear the scar
Of Christ, Anne Frank, Dreyfus,' Yevgeny said,
While KGBs were ripping David's Star.

And Yevtushenko's poem, like a *shofar*
Blew shame into the Russian soul, and dread.
They placed a statue then at Babi Yar.

The steep ravine was like a mouth gone sour
With bones and limbs and flesh it had been fed;
While KGBs tore up the yellow star.

The trees enfold the gorge like a *huppah,*
They moan a dirge and quivering leaves are shed.
There's a *menorah* now at Babi Yar;
The sun's last rays light up King David's Star.

'shofar': ram's horn, the clarion call to repentance.
'huppah': wedding canopy.
'menorah': the seven-branched candelabra.

HOUSEHOLD LINEN

*On 7 September 1938, Mussolini ordered foreign-born Jews
who had taken refuge in Italy from Germany, Poland, Austria
and elsewhere to leave the country within six months.*

He thudded his heavy case
on to my mother's polished floor,
untied the rough rope
and recited his weary litany
in a thick accent. 'I have bedlinen:

covers, double-sheets, singles, cot-sheets;
tablecloths, teacloths, traycloths – plain
and embroidered (yes madam, damask too);
bath-towels, hand-towels, guest-towels
of softest cotton, and purest lawn handkerchiefs

monogrammed. Your husband's name, madam? Jacob?
Right, six with a J in the corner. But take care
it's not J for JUDE.' And he laughed a tired laugh.
He'd taught philosophy at Heidelberg. Under the linen
he kept Kant's *Critique of Pure Reason.*

The last time he called: 'Buy the lot cheap,'
he pleaded. 'Have you seen the papers?
We can't stay here any more. So where to next?'
He fixed my mother, 'You're lucky, you're Italian.'
Her face darkened with premonition.

THE SHOUT

*Primo Levi was born and died in the same Turin
apartment block in Corso Re Umberto. The only
interruption was his time in Auschwitz.*

The *portinaia*'s voice booms up the stairwell:
'*Signora Levi, c'è suo figlio; suo figlio è qui.*'
Doors open and neighbours peer down;
who's this skeleton of a man?
Never seen *him* before.

Upstairs his mother lingers…
Can it be Primo?
But we've said *kaddish*. As a shade
from the Inferno does he come?
Or a dazzled soul from Paradiso that he loved?

She takes each step slowly.
He climbing up, they meet halfway,
not with outstretched arms
but quietly, incredulous: 'You, back from Auschwitz?'
'Yes, me. Though why me, I'll never know.'

'Why me?' was the question
that wouldn't go away;
when he went to bed at night,
in his dreams, when he got up in the morning.
'It's not my fault if I live and breathe.'

When his body was found
at the bottom of the stairwell
that April morning, forty years later,
it was at the very spot
where the *portinaia* had shouted:

'Signora Levi, your son's back from Auschwitz.'

'portinaia': concierge

43

RAILWAY TRACKS

For Lotte Kramer
who came to England from Germany in 1939
as a refugee in the 'Kindertransport'.

The child in her
still cries out to be soothed,
held close, comforted.

Staring out of the train window
she saw no fields or shady trees,
nor friendly cows or woolly sheep,
but the shadow of a mother's face,
though stern; of a father's, less so;
of a buxom maid grinding coffee
to off-key snatches of Bavarian tunes.

She wished so hard (eyes closed,
clenched fists as she did for little gifts)
that the train would accidentally stop,
run out of track and shunt backwards,
backwards 'all the way home'.

The tracks have sunk into her face.
They're lines that gather to go nowhere
save to shout her living hurt
to a page, a book, the world;
and wait for the no-answers
she blocks her ears to hear.

IDA BOROWICZ

born Russia 1920, died Entebbe Airport 1976

She had lived through the pogroms,
lived through the death camps,
lived through the labour camps.

But she died of joy at the rescue,
one dawn in an alien land – the moon still out –
when three angels dropped out of the sky,

snatched the people from their once-again persecutors
and flew them home,
her bullet-pocked body among them.

When they'd cried: 'Shalom, nobody move, it's us,'
she'd leapt up singing
and the machine-guns mowed her down.

THE DESERT WIND

For Willi Brandt 1913–1992

When the German Chancellor visited the fortress
of Masada in June 1973 his helicopter was almost
blown over the edge by a freak wind.

You didn't think, did you Willi,
that the wind would remember…
The wind can whisper but it can also howl
and up there at Masada you heard it ululate and wail;

phantoms drive it. It's an angry wind
whose unquiet hand, restless
as *the contours of the Judean hills,*
pushed your helicopter to the cliff-edge.

You stepped out pale and shaken.
Yet the Zealot wind forgave you
and gave you breath enough to say:
'I'm glad to be here.'

But the spiral of your helicopter
found no spirit echoes
in that place of scrolls.

The sea preserves in salt,
the desert in dryness
and the wind in memory.

Italicised phrases are taken from poems by the Israeli poet Yehuda Amichai.

Two Sequences

MOVEMENTS ON THE LAKE

A SONATA IN FOUR MOVEMENTS

Allegro doloroso
Scherzo
Rondo-Villanelle
Lento elegiaco

Allegro doloroso

NIGHT EXPRESS, STRESA

This mainline Milan–Lausanne express train, passing
through Stresa, was the one used by us in 1937 when
my parents decided to risk crossing the Swiss border
at Domodossola to flee Fascist Italy.

Out of the still night
the sound of a train;
it approaches, crescendoes,
dies away again. Who are
these passengers in the night,
snatched so fast, borne far?
In the mind, they stay bright
because unmet, unstopped, unknown...

But one small girl is known, ·
emerges from memory's tunnel-black:
she's asleep across a rack. DOMODOSSOLA
beats five syllables on the midnight air.
Fascist police jump aboard; they stroke her hair
but reach round her neck for the Star of David there.

'*Sono Ebrei, sono Ebrei!*' they shout
(and shout still) as the train pulls out.
It's 1937...parents and child
have crossed the border
towards life
and a new disorder.

'*Sono Ebrei*':'*They are Jews.*'

Scherzo

GRAND HÔTEL ET DES ÎLES BORROMÉES

*1935 was the year of the Stresa Conference between
Italy, France and Great Britain, held on the Borromean
island, Isola Bella. Mussolini and his entourage stayed
at the Grand Hôtel et des Îles Borromées where, as fate
would have it, my mother and I were also guests. Our
mini-conference, with an uncle from Paris, was to decide
where to go next, in the face of the increasing threat
to the Jews of Europe.*

As the guests
sipped dry Martini
in walked B'nito Mussolini.
He and other
heads of state
here in Stresa
had a date.
He'd been warned:
'Hands off the *Negus*'
(over after-dinner Stregas)
'or we'll sanction Italy
from the Alps to Sicily.'

The year was 1935 –
It was good to be alive.

We the guests
a wide aisle parted
through which flowed
the crimson carpet.
I, a tiny
girl in tulle,
stood front line
upon a stool.

As he passed
the great dictator
seeing such a small spectator
smiled and patted my
blond head
unhatted
while my mother
far behind, terrified
out of her mind,
tried to run out front
and grab me.

But by then
the party'd mounted
the wide stairs
to nurse their cares
in their linen-sheeted beds
like a group of newly-weds.

We to ours
that fateful night –
I too young
to not sleep tight.

'Negus': the name (meaning 'ruler' in the local language) used by the
Italians for Emperor Haile Selassie of Ethiopia, then Abyssinia.

Rondo-Villanelle

THE WAITER'S TALE

To eat that trout was not an easy matter
When I had heard the story that he told
(He stood – black tails, with napkin and a platter)

Of murky water, dying fish and splatter
From bayoneted women, young and old.
So eating now was not an easy matter.

I could not understand his eager chatter...
Stones around their necks and torn-off gold?
As he stood there with napkin and a platter.

Remnant of city Jews, with lives quite shattered,
Had come to shelter there, their houses sold.
(To think and eat was not an easy matter.)

'At daybreak bodies floated up,' he blattered
'Some folk would try to bury them.' Behold
Him standing there with napkin and a platter.

'But now the lake is clean; my son's a spratter.
Signora! Eat your fish, it's getting cold.'
To eat that trout became a troubling matter...
He stood – black tails, with napkin and a platter.

Lento elegiaco

AT PALLANZA

*After Badoglio's armistice with the Allies,
the Germans came down to Stresa through
the Brenner Pass. There was no time to truck
the Jews to concentration camps, so they
were put into sacks with stones round their
necks and thrown into the lake. Pregnant
women were bayoneted first.*

Now the summer's over
I'll get back into the shadows.
Scent of oleander and camellia,
and gaudy bougainvillaea
brushing against my cheek
every day on the balcony,
begins to cloy. And the too-sweet-grapes
hanging heavy from the vine,
begging to be picked, stir
dead sap in me.

Below the reflection of branches,
below the play of light,
below the light itself
down on the sands of the lake,
mixed with plankton and fish life,
are the ever-disintegrating molecules
of people just like me but not as lucky.

The stones
hung round their necks
to drag them down,
are also resting there,
below the light,
in the shadows…

Out of the sunlight
now the summer's over –
now every summer's over –
I'll stay down there
be with them
in the shadows.

RETURN TO SPAIN

A POEM WITH SEVEN BRANCHES

*to commemorate the quincentenary of the
expulsion of the Jews from Spain in 1492*

*He cerrado mi balcón
porque no quiero oir el llanto
pero por detrás de los grises muros
no se oye otra cosa que el llanto.*

Federico García Lorca

PREPARING TO LAND

Out of the window
The raked red earth
Spiked with olive trees,
Round as pin-heads
In children's games,
Rises to meet me, proclaiming
This was once my home.

I see shadows
Of Inquisitorial giants
Loom over fields of sunflowers.
On the plain of Castile
The land, long since abandoned
(Though clung-to as a mother),
Turns suddenly cold, hostile.

Yet as I near
The earth beckons
Enticing me like the hearth
Of a warm kitchen
Where people sit chatting
At ease, without reserve,
Without fear.

And I know
I have come to talk
With this land; to try and settle
The time-worn account
For those who fled
(Clutching their housekeys
In case they returned),
And for those who stayed
To face ridicule.
Gusanos the converts were called –
Worms; and *Marrano* – swine –
Still smears the apostate.

The long sing-song vowels
With gutturals and lisps
Heard in 'Arrivals',
Bring back bedtime sounds
And a bevy of aunts and cousins
Preserving the speech of Cervantes
In the intimacies of *Ladino*.

How can the words
Between me and this land
Be bitter?

'Ladino': language still spoken by Jews originating from Spain.

CYPRESSES

Three on each side of the path
To Maria Blanca of Toledo,
Stern cypresses
Shadowless at noon –
Old, perhaps planted before
The time of terror...

Are they
Six fingers pointing,
Six judges, six witnesses,
Maybe six coffins?

I cannot tell.

LONGINGS

Plaza de Juda Levi, Córdoba

Ten orange trees
In the tiny square
Called after you,
Rise like longings.

I sit under
One of them
Telling myself
Your desires:

For the Holy Land
For the stones of Jerusalem
For redemption through return
For the sacred vessels that were smashed
For the friendship of God
For healing of body and soul
For God's strong voice in your ear
For strength in old age
For snowcapped Mount Hermon
For God's hand to smooth the waves
Of the storm
That carried you to Alexandria.

On the fragrance
Of the heady blossom
I'm borne to Egypt,
Travelling your sandy road.

At the gates of Jerusalem
You lie slain
A scimitar through your heart,
Your heart still full of longing.

'Juda Levi': a major poet of the Spanish Golden Age.

ELEGY IN TOLEDO

My grandfather, whose ancestors had lived in Spain
up to the fifteenth century, died in Greece as he was
being deported from Rhodes to Auschwitz in 1944.

At the corner by El Greco's house
You, who had no house of burial,
Came to me distraught.

I knelt to touch your hand
Over the stones their hands had touched
The last time before they fled.

At the Temple, white with light,
The great oak doors trembled:
You had no burial wood.

My eyes searched the frieze
For the letter ZAIN, strength,
Among escutcheons of the House of Castile.

Father of my mother, this one-time
Jewelled city will bury you now,
A lost and murdered king;

And lay you down by these our ancestors,
By this man *'puro de manos y limpio de corazón'*;
Or this one: *'hombre ver y honorable y bueno'*.

On a rounded stone, I shall carve for you
A tree of life and Royal Peacocks –
Blue, blue and gold – so you can rend
The stone and soar to immortality.

The two Spanish headstone inscriptions read:
'Pure of hands and clean of heart';
'A good, truthful and honourable man'.

TO SYNAGOGUE – CÓRDOBA 1315

The women's feet click
And clack on the cobbles
Down narrow streets
To the newly built temple
With filigree walls.

They chatter of food
Left prepared under muslin:
Fine fila pastry
With savoury fillings,
And pale milky drinks
Made from sweet melon-pips.

The wooden stair creaks
As they climb to their eyrie
(A good vantage-point
To spot *novios* for daughters
And check the comportment
Of husbands and sons).

Framed by three arches
As candle-light flickers,
They're prettier than Marys.
Their eyes hold no tears…
These are still the good years.

STATUE OF MAIMONIDES

He sits pensive
Relaxed
On a simple stone

The much-rubbed
Embroidered slippers
Glinting in the sun.

Though dust
Covers him – today
From a building site –

No dust
Will disturb
His thoughts.

His right hand
Holds open a book,
The left grips the seat...

Does he foresee
His own
And the people's exile?

The half-turban
Spins round his head
Like a revolving planet

And the folds
Of his garment
Fall

Like the branches
Of jasmine behind him
On the cracked wall.

YOU TOO HAD A GARDEN ONCE...

'For four days the Jews were held at Haidar, again without water,
with no beds or bedding, sleeping on top of one another. A man
was dying of thirst. His name was Michel Ménaché. They gave him
urine to drink to quench his thirst. He died that afternoon.'
                                    (Martin Gilbert, *The Holocaust*)

'All this was vegetable gardens, orchards,
when I was a child,' said the girl
at the suburban bus-stop in Córdoba.

And your garden – *La Guerta* – leapt to mind;
it was outside the ghetto walls, up in the hills
in Rhodes where your forefathers laid their roots.

We had picnics there, arriving by roofless taxi
piled with food and family. The old Turk who tended it
bowed low, helped unpack, allowed us the use of his toilet.

We children ran off to climb the mulberry trees,
to pick and gorge and quench unquenchable thirsts;
then dipped our purple lips in the frolicking fountain.

Weightier fruits slaked the thirst of grown-ups (ours too):
watermelons, melons, cucumbers, lemons, oranges,
also the sweetened water from syrupy drinks.

                         *

Would I could have brought to your parched throat,
your juiceless mouth, grandfather, all the mulberries
I'd picked in my childhood, and pressed them to your lips,

that morning when the family in despair made you
drink urine. Could it be, in your delirium,
you tasted the sweet juice of watermelons?

WANDA BARFORD was born in Milan but was compelled to leave Italy in the 1930s by Mussolini's racial laws. She emigrated with her parents to Southern Rhodesia (now Zimbabwe) where she heard English for the first time. She studied Latin, Ethics and English at University College Southampton and gained her ARCM diploma from the Royal College of Music. She is married with two daughters: Jeeda, a costume designer, and Imogen, a harpist. They all live and work in London.

Initially a pianist, teacher and music critic, Wanda Barford is now pursuing her first love – poetry. Her poems have been published in a number of magazines and anthologies, and have been broadcast. She was runner-up in the H.H. Wingate/Jewish Quarterly Poetry Competition and reviews poetry for *The Jewish Chronicle*. *Sweet Wine and Bitter Herbs* is her first collection.